New York

United States

Atlantic Ocean

Panama Canal

2024 First US edition
Text copyright © 2021 by Margo Linn
Illustrations copyright © 2021 by Brian Fitzgerald

Published by Charlesbridge
9 Galen Street
Watertown, MA 02472
(617) 926-0329
www.charlesbridge.com

Originally published digitally by Blue Cat Books in 2021
All rights reserved

Library of Congress Cataloging-in-Publication Data
Names: Linn, Margo, author. I Fitzgerald, Brian, 1959– illustrator.
Title: Every here has a there: moving cargo by container ship /
    Margo Linn; illustrated by Brian Fitzgerald.
Description: First US edition. I Watertown, MA: Charlesbridge,
    2024. I Audience: Ages 3–7 I Audience: Grades K–1 I Summary:
    "A book printed in Asia makes its journey across the sea to the
    United States and into a kid's hand."—Provided by publisher.
Identifiers: LCCN 2023033799 (print) I LCCN 2023033800
    (ebook) I ISBN 9781623544843 (hardcover) I ISBN
    9781632894274 (ebook)
Subjects: LCSH: Container ships—Juvenile literature. I Shipment
    of goods—Juvenile literature.
Classification: LCC HE566.C6 L56 2024 (print) I LCC HE566.C6
    (ebook) I DDC 387.5/442—dc23/eng/20230815
LC record available at https://lccn.loc.gov/2023033799
LC ebook record available at https://lccn.loc.gov/2023033800

Printed in China
(hc) 10 9 8 7 6 5 4 3 2 1

Display type set in Canvas 3D Sans by Ryan Martinson
Text type set in Mr Hand by Mightyfire
Printed by 1010 Printing International Limited in Huizhou,
    Guangdong, China
Production supervision by Jennifer Most Delaney
Designed by Ellie Erhart

EVERY HERE HAS A THERE

MOVING CARGO BY CONTAINER SHIP

Margo Linn

Illustrated by Brian Fitzgerald

ini Charlesbridge

Here we are in Asia. Lots of book boxes are leaving a factory to be trucked to the port of Hong Kong, China.

Every **HERE** has a **THERE**.

Every **CLOSED** has an **OPEN**.

The boxes will be unloaded from the truck, stacked on pallets, and sorted by their final destination.

They are then placed into shipping containers.

The books are now ocean freight and will be loaded onto a huge container ship.

Every **UP** has a **DOWN**.

Every **QUIET** has a **NOISY**.

A crane lifts the full containers up, and over, and down onto the deck of the giant ship.

Containers are piled one on top of another. A stack might be taller than an apartment building!

Inside the containers are cartons packed with computers, chemicals, electronics, machinery, tools, books, toys, clothing—almost anything!

Every **HIGH** has a **LOW**.

Every **TOGETHER** has an **APART**.

A container ship is full when there is no more space above or below deck. The ship will not leave the harbor until it is fully loaded with 5,000 or more containers.

Getting a ship fully loaded takes at least a week, sometimes longer.

Every **BOW** has a **STERN**.

Does every **FRONT** have a **BACK**?

The captain has a command center high up on the ship. It's called the bridge.

It holds more navigation machinery than you can imagine. It's enough to guide the ship on the long trip across the ocean.

Once the ship is in the open ocean, the captain can start the engine, turn up the throttle, and speed up.

Every **EMPTY** has a **FULL.**

Every **LARGE** has a **SMALL**.

Tugboats point the bow of the ship out toward the Pacific Ocean.

It's "all hands on deck." The twenty or more people with different jobs on the ship are ready to begin work.

When the crew has breaks, they can watch movies and TV, exercise in the gym, eat meals in the cafeteria, or rest in their rooms.

The ship is their home for the next month, and it's got to be comfortable!

Every **PULL** has a **PUSH.**

Every **OFF** has an **ON**.

The ship's deck is above the water line. The deck is loaded with containers. And each one is tied down.

Below deck is the belly of the ship. It's also fully loaded with containers. And it has all the machinery and engines that are necessary to propel the ship forward.

The ship will take a four-week journey.

Every **ABOVE** has a **BELOW.**

Every **DAY** has a **NIGHT**.

The captain navigates from the bridge. He's on the lookout for other ships and for storms.

The captain must guide the ship not only when the weather is good, but also when it is bad.

The waves rock and roll the ship up and down. The ocean highway can be bumpy! And containers can fall off into the sea if they haven't been properly tied down.

Every **LIGHT** has a **DARK**.

Does every **LOUD** have a **SOFT**?

The ship crosses the Pacific Ocean.

The hours and days pass slowly.

The port of New York is still far, but the Panama Canal is near.

Every **FAR** has a **NEAR**.

Every **EAST** has a **WEST**.

Instead of going the long way around South America and Cape Horn, the ship takes a shortcut through the Panama Canal.

This is the shortest distance to New York. It saves time, fuel, and money!

Every **LONG** has a **SHORT**.

Every **WIDE** has a **NARROW.**

The ship arrives at the Panama Canal. It waits in line.

The canal is an engineering wonder. It allows the ship to pass from the Pacific Ocean to the Atlantic Ocean. A series of canal locks help transport the ship across the Isthmus of Panama.

The ship travels through the canal for about twelve hours before it comes out the other side.

Every **SOUTH** has a **NORTH**.

Every **STOP** has a **GO**.

The ship spends another week sailing north in the Atlantic Ocean.

The seas are often rough on the way to New York. It can sometimes be a difficult journey.

Every **CALM** has a **ROUGH.**

Does every **SAFE** have an **UNSAFE?**

The captain and crew wave hello to the Statue of Liberty in New York.

Now the captain is faced with a problem. How will he park a giant ship at a crowded port? Short answer: it's complicated!

The captain gets expert help from tugboats and other workers, who are in charge of parking all the boats that enter the port.

Every **DEPARTURE** has an **ARRIVAL.**

Every **TOP** has a **BOTTOM.**

After a month on the ocean, the ship is ready to be unloaded.

Cranes hoist containers off the ship. Dock workers sort the cargo and send the containers to different places on the pier.

Next the containers are unpacked and the boxes are sent to port storage.

Paperwork for each shipment is sent to a customs office, where it is checked. The officers decide whether the goods are safe and legal and can enter the USA.

Every **LOAD** has an **UNLOAD.**

Every **LEFT** has a **RIGHT.**

Here we are at a bookstore.

The book boxes went from the pier to a warehouse. Then they were delivered to this store in small trucks.

The books are unpacked, sorted, and shelved so they are ready for shoppers.

Every **IN** has an **OUT**.

Every **THERE** has a **HERE**.

The books are organized by type so kids can find them easily. Some categories might be board books, picture books, easy-reader books, chapter books, graphic novels, and more.

There might be display tables for other kinds of books: series, bestsellers, and coloring books.

Where in the store do you find your favorite books?

Every BOOK has a READER.

Does every **READER** have a **BOOK**?